I0108947

Gifts of Grace

Vivian Kearney

Gifts of Grace
©2020, Vivian Kearney
Cover illustration © 2020, Vivian Kearney
Pukiyari Publishers

The total or partial reproduction of this book is prohibited. This book cannot be totally or partially reproduced, transmitted, copied or stored using any means or ways including graphic, electronics or mechanic without the consent and written authorization of the author, except in the case of small quotes used in articles and written comments about the book.

ISBN-13: 978-1-63065-133-6

PUKIYARI PUBLISHERS
www.pukiyari.com

Dedicated to God
with prayers for His creation and creatures

*With thanks to God
for life, love, Milo, our families, friends,
graces more than galore and
for Ani Palacios McBride,
our friendly, helpful and very patient editor*

Table of Contents

Our Nature

Star Stuff

Star stuff
We are made of star dust

Look at our ancestors'
Beginnings

Way back
Deep in space

Your great-grandparents'
Shining radiance

Your grandparents –
Like protostars
Your parents
Blue / white
Supernova

And now
On this chattering planet

Your Father wants
To talk to you
Talking to Him

Everlasting face
To star-lit face
Creator to created

Autobiographer

It takes
More than a lifetime
To write
A true autobiography

To include
Every moment

And more
Than another lifetime
To write, read and understand
Another person's
Life story

With all its nuances
Layers, stages and aspects

Only God has all the time
And does

Sliding Scales

We each dwell
On sliding scales

Of OCD, ADD, Asperger's
PTSD, *mishigene shtik*
(eccentric tics)

As societies
Keeps shifting
The categories
To make up
New normals

Translating, analyzing
Trying to fixate
Behaviors

While every person
Sails on their individual river
Searching for the ocean
Warm and endless

Of God's love

You Are

Not a number
Choosing paths

Predicted
By sociological maps

But an individual
None like you

With unique ways
Of travelling your own road

Accompanied
Or met by
God-sent angels
Of redemption

Immeasurable – Luke 7:30

It's
Not a waste
Of our hoarded emotions, ruminations

To offer them all
To God – Creator
Savior, Holy Spirit

To check the desktop
Chat rooms and e-mails
Dwelling in
Our computer-like minds

And ask Him
To rewire our souls
To His transcendent
High definition
Communication

Much as
Did the woman
Gifting that precious ointment

With her
Immeasurable gratefulness
For His
Infinite grace

Multi-hued Facets

The rhythms of the writing waves
The messages on the worried page
The smiles of colorful sunsets
The revisited sapphire caves

The kaleidoscopes of forests
The kind promises to keep
The poems of the past
The dreams illegibly deep

Those and more facets of our lives
Lord, help us offer for Thy kingdom
For Thine be the glory and crowns
Thine the way, the light and the wisdom

Lamentations, John

Our steps are painful, our hopes few
Our smiles more precious than deserts' dews
We cry for miracles, yet when they are sent
We waste time in mistaken arguments

The Lord God is greater than the earth's cares
And exceeds the boundaries of our despair
Lord, give us the grace and strength to look above
Our burdens and crosses to Thy skies of love

To Find Out

What sadness to find out
The color of the skin is unwanted
The line of kin is mysterious
The feared night doesn't turn to daylight
The charismatic leader doesn't guide right
The hopeful goals were wrong
And there is no place
For the soul's song

What happiness to find out
Every color is beautiful
God is our Father bountiful
There are many ways He tells us
To take care of the world
He loves to help, bless and redeem
We can be inspired, comforted by His word
He leads us to good goals, peace, helpfulness
Let's applaud God's presence and His grace

Arranging and Rearranging

Arranging and rearranging
Plans, things and thoughts
On God's given planet

That seems to be
Our Sisyphean chore
Ever moving burdens, schedules
To have them roll down
Once more

But on the shores
Of our desiring
In the *barrio*
Of our dreams
Above our streams
Of consciousness

Rules God – our Savior
O understand
Wisdom-seeking man

We are not doomed to
A meaningless existence
When He offers us His hand

Who Is Always With You?

You are always with you
A collection of conundrums

God is always here with you
A light and many a healing song

Habits and Algorithms – *The Economist* – June 19, 2020, p. 68

Habits are algorithms
Brains are partly
Statistical machines
Prompted by dog whistles
Where does the human soul
Live in all this?

The soul wants to move
Out of the cave of materialism
And asks Jesus to walk alongside
Lift burdens, renew hopes and guide
Us when we cry

Would faith slip-slide away
With loaded words, stormy days?

Would His forgiveness heal
And healing be granted
Along with redeemed attitudes?

Will cathedrals be rebuilt
With born again beginnings
Worshipping God with gratitude?

Warning and Advice

A peeve is not a pet, you know
It starts off small, but then it grows
Into a devouring lion who roams
Around your heart, your soul and home

Better to remember His gifts of grace
How you and others were mercifully blessed
By the King of the infinite starry cosmos
Who offers forgiveness and healing from the cross

Mixed Messages on TV

Look, here's a presentation
About Jesus' life
Of miracles and lessons
About selflessness

Yet wait –
For the interrupting commercials
Our cool, promising
Modern money changing tables

Behold this double vision
Persuasive advertising
For a materialistic life
Mixed into Jesus' teaching

Heeding the Line

Lord, what is the line, the crossover
From gratefulness to smugness
From joy for surprising gifts of grace
To triumphal pride and self-righteousness

Lord, thank you for Thy Counseling Holy Spirit
Keeping us from exulting presumptions
And for walking us past valleys of mistakes
Please help our spirits closer to Thee wake

Greater Than Our Stardust Minds

We can look at the stars
Looking at God

We can cooperate peaceably
On our individual journeys
Towards heaven

We can find meaning
Above triumphalism
Through clues

Here, on just the right planet
In this, beyond awesome universe

Made and being shaped by
Our individual-loving Creator

Greater than
Our stardust minds
Can describe

Though we can sing
Hallelujah

Yad VaShem – Hand and Name

When the
Alphabet of our lives
Is near its end
And we tend
To drop some memories
Syllables
And syllabi

Let us remember
And honor Thy mercies,
Thy hand – deeds and lessons,
Thy holy names, Lord
That stretch our numbered letters
To forever
Beyond these skies

Bounties Bestowed

Gifts of Grace

Flowers of wonder
Gifts of grace
O for the love
To seek His face

Awakening Alarm

Dawn's light
Through the window blinds
My gentle alarm

We Didn't Have to Have

We didn't have to have light
For this shadowed world

We didn't have to have love
Above our striving

We didn't have to have rainbows
Of hope skipping through clouds

We didn't have to have beauty
Murmuring beyond sadness

We didn't have to have Creation at all
Nor the Christ child Who calls

Us at Christmas
And in each season

Yet, amazingly
We do

Today

Today I wrote one poem
Sang two songs
Prayed three prayers
Gave four thanks
Did five quite good deeds

However, I received
Countless blessings
Starbursts of wonder
Miracles of grace

Glory be
For God's immeasurable
Unearned bounty

May All Receive

A smell of England in the air
Birds flying high, velvet flowers fair
A memory of being tourists in a far land
Free as children from time's demands

Lord, Thou hast given us such good things
Family, friends and senses giving hearts wings
To rejoice in Thy grace continually
Lord, may all suffering ones also comforted be

Providential – After book –
***A Street Cat Named Bob* – by James Bowen**

Street musician in London
Strumming for his bread
Meets an amazing street cat
Just as needy

And they loyally
Take good care of each other
Entertaining, greeting many
On the sidewalks
Of the busy city

If that isn't
A lovely witness
Of unexpected
Providential grace

What is?

Then There is the Personal

Then there is the personal
Matter of a car
In front of mine
Maddeningly stalled

Why didn't it move?

In my haste
I deemed it an annoying
Setback

That driver wasn't looking
Or was snoozing, texting
Definitely
Not on the alert

But lo and behold
Out of my vision, turning the corner
Was a vehicle that would have crashed
If everything had gone as I asked

The providential pauses
Detours, stalls and stops

How many times
Did that happen?

A Blessed Visit

It is a historic occasion
My mother said

Your landing from the clouds
To meet again

Talking in the forever
Familiarity and love

And mostly
Sunlit memories

Matchmaker

I take you as you are
You take me as I am
We give each other
Time, conversation, care
Comfort, love

At every stage
Of our glad lives
Together

Brought together, kept together
By the heavenly grace
Of our matchmaking Father

Pre-Sleep

As
I wander down
Narrow dark halls
Of pre-sleep
I touch the walls
And behold

At every contact
A memory screen lights up
A technicolor
Mini-documentary
Complete with
Voice-over commentary

Then
Jesus walking ahead of me
Opens the door
At the end of the corridor
To a wavy shore

Ushering the unknown horizons
Of a lovely sleep sea

They Try

Flowers try
To inspire
Glad wonder

Trees try
To donate shade
And clean the air for all

Clouds try
To bring enough rain
For our thirsty earth

The moon tries
To dance with us
In gravity's rhythm

Stars try
To wink their lights
Through darkness

Pets try
To talk to us
With empathy

Birds try
To help us look above

God tries
To reach us with His love

Lent for Safekeeping

This pet
And these objects
That you've left with us
That we keep in trust
Happily

Show a little
Of how much
We love you
Dear family

Just so
This earth's beauty
God has lent us
For safekeeping

Lit by
The sun by day
The moon and stars by night
Plus promising rainbows
And northern lights

Show a little
Of how much
God loves us

Welcomed to the Free Light Show

You can only see
The free light show
Of stars dancing with the moon
When you look up to
The night heavens

Otherwise
The pale blue skies
Of being on the privileged
Winning side
Of the day

Blinds you
To the tiny twinkling
Empathy-conveying
Winks of grace
From above

BC / AD

Before Christ talked to me
I thought I was beholden

To beauties in creation
And arts all around
While I wandered haphazardly
Seeing what I could find
In the museum of my mind

Now through
Strange grace
I can visit
With the Curator-Creator
And give Him glad thanks
For also being
Father-Savior

What Language?

How did He speak to me?
What language did He use?

It was a light that was a door
Beyond a Montreal flat

It was a cloud
Of heather from the Brontes

It was an audible voice
Introducing me to Milo
In Latin class
In maple-leafed Montreal

It was an encouraging
Cooling and sparkling
Waterfall dream
In an attic room
Of flower-child Berkeley

It was a prophetic dream
Of children before they were born

It was a vision before baptism
In palm-treed Brownsville
And a double rainbow
To celebrate with after

It was a white dove alighting
On a steepled cross
On a little church
On a hill

It was many a whispered warning
On the road

A million remembered
Talks, rides and walks

And a warm smile in my heart
Recalling many granted prayers

Little by Little

Who Sent Them? Who Made Them?

If angels came into your life, Who sent them?
If beauties cheer all around, Who made them?
If serendipity and synchronicity and plain good luck
Skip into your life
Who timed their spontaneous dances just right?

Each person can only walk one step at a time
Each wonder should be meditated on
Only God above can mend the world
To build His kingdom
Of beauty, peace, healing, truth and love

Dispensational Ladder

Thank you God, Holy Father
For these steps of paper
Where I can run up and down
The days and years

Where Thou didst speak
Little by little, incrementally
Through windows and doors
Wonders and fears
On pages, some now yellowing
Scattered and tattered

O hold me, balance me
To keep moving, climbing farther
Closer, o closer to Thee

Getting Used To

Dear Abba
I love that Thou

Lightest the blue dawn
So gradually
Beautifully and considerately
Dispensationally

So that our souls' retinas
Can get used to
Thy dazzling sun

Managing

Don't
Get angry
At *chronos* time

The seconds slipping,
The minutes meandering
The hours hurrying,

The days disappearing
The weeks wandering
The months marching
The years yelling

That you're getting older

Chronos is managing
Your world
Running ahead
Of his cousin, *kairos*

Who will
Open the gates
To heaven's timelessness

Dispensed Grace in the Morning

Little by little
Step by slow step
The night cedes
The dark blue becomes
Royal, then lighter
Through the blinds
And the yawning walls
Wake up with the dawn

Little by little
Step by unsure step
Insights light
The way to forgiveness

Ancient bitterness
Of hidden war years cedes
To thankfulness
For what appears
With the morning sun

String Theory

God made strings first of all
So that later-created people could hear
Melodies strummed by
The Holy Spirit

And, much later
Try to harmonize
With earth grown wiser
Offering to God
Honoring songs

Guitar Sounds Coming Round

Once
I crossed a darkened bridge
Alone on a rainy, starless evening
From a quiet small country capital
To an even quieter, smaller French town

To a folk-singing café
Echoes of guitar melodies
Strumming my solitary heartstrings
With shivering foreshadowings

Whispering to me
Something spiritual
But I didn't understand
Yet

Years later
A sweet beginning
Guitar playing grandson
Also his brother, cousins
Earnestly played
Thanks for amazing graces

Then I heard and joined
Communal musical worship
Of church services

God speaking to me
In the past, in the present

Now I understand
And believe

Collected Artworks

A ringbinder for
Each once baby-sat grandchild
Step by step their art

Time Budges – *Dee Tzeit Rikt Zeech*

Time budges
Dee tzeit rikt zeech
Minute by minute
Second by second
Like clocked clouds

Inch by inch
Like an escalator
Or moving sidewalk

Propelling this planet
And this body
Both getting older

I wonder how
I did so much
Before

Time budges
And I need
To budget it
I don't want to fall
In the spaces left

And at the end
Of this earth trip
Please let me keep
Holding Thy hand, Lord

And Milo's
And family's

Praying for them
And neighbors
And friends

Gradually

If we want our souls
To fly in spiritual realms
With God

First we have to
Swim in the stream of time
Navigate with the jewelled
Fishes of moments and hours

Then crawl onto the beaches
Of busy goals

To walk in the foothills of inspiration
Hiking on His mountains of spices

And fly as high as the eagles
With the mercies of Christ

How I Found Out About Christmas

Carols in Protestant public school classes
Learning and loving the melodies, hinted mysteries
Home folks not thrilled at all, irritated
By my constant chanting other culture words

Sparkling snow sculptures
And transparent ice castles
Of McGll in the winter
Wandering around Montreal
With my grace-met
Christian soul mate

Walks home from campus
Up the hilly slope of Cote St Catherine
Where opulent perched houses
Sported live pine trees outside, in the snow
Each with a different uni-colored glow
For me, jealously outside the imagined warmth

Balmy, mostly hippy California town
Invited to a friend's family party
Given a small gift unexpectedly
Telling her I appreciate
This exotic holiday

Celebrated fully at last inside
With kids' pageants and church ceremonies
Finally realizing the Christmas reason –
Jesus, Lord of this and all seasons

Needed Pilgrimage

Time and life
Are on a trajectory   .
Undeniably

As soon as we can
We hike on a trail,
A hill, a bridge or mountain range
Or sail moving waters, fly inspiring skies
With some goal, always

Many's the rest stops
To enjoy or deploy
Especially in golden years

But our minds
Want to more forward to explore
And create paths for others

And our souls want to continue
Our pilgrimage here and beyond
Journeying forever
Towards and with God

God Is; God Does

He Is

Forgiveness is understanding
Understanding is love, Who is
God – ever-present here
And in heaven above

Conundrum, Later

What came first
The chicken or the egg?

I always am
Says the Creator
Let's talk about conundrums
Later

God Knows

The alphabet of each creation, issue
God knows
For He is the Alpha and Omega

While we may see unending circles
Of vapors and vanities
Veiling various presents

God sends encouragement, family, friends
Walking us through crises, cruelties
Hardships, sickness, persecution

He arranges an answering language
With a biblical view
Of hopes renewed

Torn the Veil

Once deterministic were gods of old
Who wove, distributed fates of souls
Jesus rent those webs apart
Offering a new road, a fresh start

Now fatalistic are we about our DNA
Deciding we'll end up in a specific way
Jesus gave us a kinder ladder
So we could all meet our good Father

Write a poem with the Writer
Create a picture with the Painter
Sing your prayers with God constantly
Join His unpredictable artistry

Brought To Us By

Existence He creates
Friendship He sends
Rests He offers
Meaning He grants

Steps we take
Words we decide
Questions we ask
Schedules we try

Caves we cherish
Opinions we hold
Happiness we chase
Eternity we hope

Since God exists forever
We can abide by His divine side
His light, path and love
Be our trusted, eternal guide

Creation, Redemption

If it were all so easy
What would be
God's glory?

The Good Listener

God – the good Listener
So present you can't dim
His memory away

God Placed

The charismatic lamp in the sky
Our planet orbits pleasantly plus
The lesser, peaceful orb
That circles quietly around us

God, the Master Electrician
Also scattered some glitter
To sparkle the night, giving
This and much more in trust

That we appreciate these gifts
And care for fellow creations
And not grind down our neighbors
Or galaxy into capitalistic dust

Above and Beyond

Above the river
Sparkling silver
In perpetual motion
Rushing to oceans

Over cherished particulars
Lovely happenings and wonders
That too quickly
Change depressingly

Beyond the stars glorious
Shines the numinous
Way to the Creator
Divine Guide and Father

Temples may disappear
Yet He stays truly near
Personal and forever
Holy Spirit, Abba, Savior

Eclipse Today

That the smaller moon
Can blot out the sun, our huge star
Is astonishing, is amazing enough

Then, that the sun
By degrees
By God's decree

Would predictably
Return to us

Is more than enough
To inspire a world-wide
Hallelujah chorus

Mark 8:27-29

Who do people say I am?
What is their worshipping plan?
Tolerance, love, inclusion and charity
Or a self-righteous fortress mentality?

Lord, where in the world art Thou
When we try to hold Thee to the here and now
Yearning to keep a child's sweet faith
While with our grown minds meditate

On Thy goodness and holiness
Thy name we know we should bless
Thy steps are seen, but not Thy face
We can't arrange, categorize Thy grace

In these kaleidoscopic changeable lands
Let us reach for Thy guiding hand
Knowing there are no gods except Thee
Let us pray for Thy kingdom, peace and glory

Fatalism Versus Salvation

It is what it is
Can't fix it
Don't go there

To repeat
It is what it is
Because it was what it was
Back to
The beginning of time

Lord, please free us
From determinism's
Uncharitable chains
Or predestination's
Unmoving frame
Or cynicism's
Distracting games
Or fatalism's
Pessimistic ties

…..

 – That's why
I came

To restart
Your heart

To redeem
The earth

With a spiritual
Rebirth

The Later Picture

A picture of a man taking a picture
Of a house now for a different family
Its angles still foreboding
Although not too revealing

Except to those he told
Of the unlove, the uncaring
The sadistic games in the name
Of bitterness untamed

Little child inside, God saw
He took you out, gave you a camera
To take a photograph from the car
With a later, closer family, far
From the unfair, convoluted pain

For we are
Given commissions to other generations
While God heals us with gifts
Of work, wonder, love, wisdom
To relay help from His kingdom

Clue Giver

God is indeed
The revealer of secrets
By His Holy Spirit
We are informed
As He sees fit

Father, Thou hast arranged
Exactly, providentially
Conditions to somewhat
Resolve mysteries
When a clue to my histories
Was revealed

With a portentous little brown suitcase
With personal papers
Found in one home
With quiet talks near picture windows
Occurring in another
Later a translator of the found document
Telling me
What city was my birthplace

And those other stories built so carefully
Came tumbling down
Now may many thanks abound
For some histories found
And to Thee be all praise and glory

Close Enough to Follow

Will the real Jesus
Stand in the river
Walk in our marketplace
Worship at our temple

Or will He turn into a distant star
Viewing us from afar
Can we truly talk to Jesus – God incarnate
As a best friend, a rabbi

Will our real souls follow Him
(Whom good angels once announced)
To shoulder caring ministries and hear
With empathy our neighbor's deepest stories

It's Your Turn

Birds, it's your turn
To be observed

With your beautiful
Amazing feathers

Artistic flights of fancy
From our Lord, Creator?

Bridge Over Troubled Waters

God is the Comforter
The world – not so much
He suffers the torturous
Cross for us

God is the meaning
Of the flesh and blood sacrament
So we can remember
More than doctrinal words

God is the Sender
Of missionaries and mentors
Messengers of His care
Here and everywhere

Yet He cannot be seen
He can't be touched
He doesn't dwell in buildings

But we can meet Him

On the bridge of love

Flower Prompts

God spoke
And there were flowers
With wonderful colors
For their clothes

We can
Appreciate them
And talk about
His amazing technicolor
Other creations on this
Goldilocks planet

And arrange
Our own bouquets
Of peace, kindness
Helpfulness, joy
Gratefulness, patience
And self-control

To adorn the temple
Of the Creator
And His Holy Spirit
Bless

River of Rests

Synchronicity
Serendipity
Or is it grace

Flights of contemplation
Walks of meditation
Rambling ruminations
By the river
The river of rests

Ripples reflecting
Lights refracting
Breezes rejuvenating
These minutes blessed

Brought by
God Who knows
Where all rivers flow
And can sail each soul
On every wavy crest

God Is; God Does

God is
The Father, Creator
Who cares

God does
All sorts of wonders
Including leading

Us to redemption,
Forgiveness,
Commissions

And He does
Love us

Time's Witness

Time will show
And time will tell
What our souls
Know very well

God searches for us
As we look for Him
With love's trust
Though ways be dim

Then with His Holy Spirit
We can choose ministries
O Lord may we be attuned
To Thy music everlastingly

And If

And if I can't
God knows

And if I won't
God redirects

And if I try
God helps

And if I trust
God talks

Signs and Offers

There They Are

There it is
The mysteriously winding
Veiled and shining
Bible for us to meet
Ancient people and God

There it is
The x-ray of a cloth
With evolving confirmations
By our improving scientific scrutiny
Of God's suffering

There it is
This marbled earth
The world with a cast of billions
These continual gifts
We are given to cherish

There it is
This ephemeral life

There He is
Our invisible God
Who gives us
Evidenced grace

Offer

– Let Me help you
Make lemonade out of lemons

Via stormy clouds
To bring nourishing rain

To fashion luminescent pearls
Out of irritating, annoying
Gravel and sand

Then we'll plant the beginning
Of another Garden of Eden
In your thoughts

Chazak Ve-iematz - **Be Strong and of Good Courage**

– But I battle more shadows than others
Leftovers from childhood and war

– Don't fear; all is not lost
I, your Abba can send you mercies and rhymes
And I am with you past the end of time

Our Continents Mirrored Above

Grey pillowy masses
In the dark, ponderous sky

Created and accumulated
Molecules of moisture
Falling upward

Those clouds seem to retain
The shapes of earth's continents
Whence they came

Remind us to remember
Landed smiles, tears
Myriad prayers all over
Against legions of pains

What Happens After

What happens
When your persona fades and shreds

And there you're left
Without a mask

Sans podium

But with lazy habits
Searching for a new spirit

Maybe God can get through
With His messages

Delivered in a car
Called serendipity

Clearing a road
Once given up

With directions
Lettered anew

In a language of signs
Known only to you

A Dream

A dream

How do you capture
Its insights in symbols
To keep in real life
Its truth from another realm?

A dream

What do you do with it
Did someone send it?
Should you let it evaporate
Into more needed sleep?

A dream

Who was in it – before unseen
Or once present – are they still communicating
With their continuing discussions
Where to address your answers?

A dream

May its contents be remembered
May its characters be blessed
May its message be discerned
May its commission be followed

If it be
For God's glory and goodness
In truth, wisdom and kindness

Countdown to Sleep

Leave those heavy day nets
On the beaches of evening
All that business, those burdens
And follow Me through

Amazing imaginary architecture
Green flowered fields
Where you can count
My goodwill sheep

And there will be peace
And healing sleep

Present Forever

There will be
No more
Date same number
Times three

That ended
On 12/ 12/ 2012

Though,
Not to worry
God is still
The Holy Trinity

Father, Son and Holy Spirit
Present eternally

At Dawn

At dawn, down the street
The sun lends its golden rays
To the tops of green trees

Day's Play

Coos and chirps in trees
This early morning

Electricity or birds?

Man-made marvels or
The beginning of
Nature's musical theatre?

We've All Been Looking For

Those silver linings
We've been looking for
Battling against dark clouds
Of discouragement

May not
Keep glimmering forever

May float away
On their calendar clouds

Though now
Those half-hidden reasons
For some continued optimism

Can also be seen
As golden rays
From the sun beckoning
Through grey days

Sunflowers Hugging

Sunflowers you gave
Press against the window pane
Hugging the sunlight

How to Translate This Answer

While I was
Watering the dry grasses
The brown and yellow patches
And thirsty weeds

Activated by
Media's promise
Of another hot and sunny
Two weeks

I asked God
What scheduling efforts
Should be pledged today

Then a miniature feather
Light and lovely
Floated cozily
Into my free hand

And I wondered
How to translate
This little, whimsical
Sign from above

Divine Daring

The bravery of the heavens
The nobility of the stars
The courage of the winds
The strength of the oceans

Together they help us realize
God's divine daring
In combining souls with bodies
To take loving care of
His creation

Ce Matin - This Morning

Ce matin
J'ai ramassé
Une petite serviette blanche

Que je croyais
Etait brodée
D'un cactus

Mais c'était celle
Avec deux coeurs enlacés
Des fleurs

(Comme mon ami le plus cher,
Milo et moi)

Alors la vie
Ne consiste pas
Seulement des cactus
Qui percent nos doigts
Et nos rêves

L'amour et les espoirs
Reviennent, renaissent
Toujours

Avec de petits
Ou de grands signes

Grâce au Bon Dieu
Notre Bon Dieu d'amour

This morning

This morning
I picked up
A little white towelette

That I thought
Was the one embroidered
With a cactus

But it was actually
The one decorated with
Two hearts intertwined
With flowers

(Like my dearest friend, Milo and I)

So life doesn't only
Consist of cacti
That pierce our fingers
And our dreams

Love and hopes
Come back, revive always
With tiny or great signs

Thanks to the good Lord
Our good God of love

Metaphors, Rhythms and Rhymes

Words are
Stop-motion
Photography
Sometimes getting together
To record passing time
In poetry

Similes gather
Elements together
Metaphors even more so
While with
Rhythms, rhymes, alliteration
Melodious carpets are fashioned

God, Thou art
The ultimate poet
Creating poems within poems
Planet earth within galaxies
Galaxies within the universe

With ecosystems as rhymes
Rhythms of day, night and seasons
Oceans dancing to gravity
And the appointed
Peaceful moon
Bowing to the messenger Son

Stardust Came Down

Stardust came down
And kissed the earth
To lend its colors
To the sky and flowers

Jesus came down
And walked the earth
To spread forgiving light
On our shadowed world

Churches

Joseph's Coat

A coat of many colors
A cloth rainbow
To wear, to enlighten
Souls around
With hope's clothes
For infinite tomorrows

A prayer shawl
Blue and white
To know God's arms
Are sheltering us
From storms of worries
Sands of prejudice
Winds of sadness
Helping to receive
And share His grace

A consecrated meal
A communion with our Teacher
A change of heart
A renaissance
Celebrating with
A numinous tune
Guiding us
Home

Church at Night

Gratefully we thank Thee
For the church at night
Wonderfully lit, colors bright
Stained glass windows beautiful
Metaphors for Thy art

Not So Empty

Songs float, notes trip merrily
Piano sounds dance slowly or quickly
In the practicing church
Mainly deserted except for the choir

But maybe not so empty

Just as a half-full glass
Is not really half-vacant
Since the air
Is also there

The witnessing building
Can be considered whole
By the listening heavens
And some hushed workers
And a few lone visitors

Mainly because
The Holy Spirit
Of Jesus, God
Might be breathing,
Walking, praying
There

Parish Hall

All are welcome
Welcome in this place
Where our spirits can talk
About God's amazing grace

Where crosses on the wall speak
Speak to each seeking soul
With varied patterns teaching
Christ's story new and old

Where we and the candles
Candles of inspiration
Can sing with the music
Songs of God's salvation

Rejoice with the wonders
Wonders of the great oak trees
Every season for every reason
Praising God gratefully

If Read in Order
(according to *The Witness of the Stars*
by E. W. Bullinger)

On the church screen
The holy family manger scene
While background sparkles
With happy stars intermittently

The constellation-like pattern
If read in order, symbolically
Can tell the gospel story

Glints of Bullinger's theory?

Church Retreat

Lamps reflect into infinity
Through clear windows
Of walls open on three sides
To the gray heavens, green hills

Tears of rain
Wash the statue of Jesus
Tall as the trees
Walking the earth
With arms outstretched

Iron the hands that sign
Loving mercies

While we commune
In this country church
Of tawny carpets
Reassuring stone
Quieting wood

Inspired by
Vistas past vistas
Telling us, singing with us:
Look on Christ
Reconnect with
Your Savior

Retreat Prompts

The plush camel with proud red-green-Christmassy
tassels
Is laden with kettle, pots, packages, blankets
All for others, but what about its own needs?

Are we supposed to accept those symbolic provisions
Of helpfulness, sent by God
Carried on metaphorical camels
To wander with what faith through what deserts?

Some parcels carry obviously
Useful gifts, shining,
Reflecting His light

Others may require some
Explanations and
Untying

Once a Hill Country Evening

Lovely the sunset over the hills
Beyond oak trees with their
Artistically curved branches

The horizon's farewell hues of pinkish peach
Hovering over the bluish-green mountains
White and mauve wildflowers answering

Quiet our time for writing exercise
Are the trees writing too
With the sky as their paper

Rosy-cheeked baby appreciating our lesson
By slapping and chewing the
Instruction booklet

Utterances of joyful approval
From a mute teen in a wheelchair

Jesus looking at us
From His portrait
Talking in each one's language

How lovely is this meditating evening
Diving down, down, down for

Our voices under the mountains
Through the flowing branches of trees
Rewriting the patterns
Of the multi-colored
Meditational carpet

Church Program – The Bible and Broadway

Great plush lion
Majestically maned
Streamlined, lithe
Royally stands
On the stage-prop
Bible

His names:
Aslan, Cecil, Simba, Lion-King

Our test question:
Can we bring our pop culture's
Iconic symbols
Into our praying lives?

Christmas Presentation

Little girl
Play angel
Leading us, telling us
To worship the baby Jesus

Represented by
A doll in a stage stable
For a Christmas musical

While in the audience
A real baby's cry
Is heard

And others intercede
For many miracles
For healings needed

By everyone's
Year-round Savior

Church Before Christmas

The shuffling dry leaves
Orange, brown, red, gold
Like bits of a puzzle
Blown by the wind

Seem color-coded
But who knows the message
And planned the key
And what's the big picture?

The fresh southwestern day
Autumn-cool in winter
Energized by practiced music
Interspersed with pauses
Softly preparing a path
For the advent
Of the Holy Child

Scattered lights
Of Christmas gladness

O that they would
Glitter through the years
With dancing, carpeting leaves

Blue and White Canopy

A *talit*, spread the *talit*
The blue and white
Prayer shawl
High over the heads
Of fellow congregants
At the service

And keep holding
A virtual shawl
Over everyone
In our thoughts
And beyond
All families, friends,
Acquaintances, neighbors

A *talit* of prayer, concern
For salvation, protection, help,
Healings

As Thou, Lord spreadest
The blue sky and white clouds
Over Thy creatures
To comfort, bless

After a Messianic Service

After the service, some tinkling piano notes
Played by children occupying the stage
In the now emptying sanctuary

Where just before, murmured hopes wafted
Over stretched prayer shawls –
Momentary homes

Protecting neighbors, families, together
Lord, let not one soul be left alone

On a Church Screen

What will our souls look like
Dancing in the heavens
Skipping among galaxies

Will we be
Perfectly proportioned cubes
Or floating circles
Rough edges smoothed

Or still dwell
In our familiar earth shapes
Bodies healed, minds joyfully
Discussing His creation
With our Father

The Creator of past, present
And eternity

Tell Us During the Service

We are here
To worship God
To get close to our Savior
And praise our Redeemer

In this thin
And beautiful place
He lends us
We built for Him
In thankfulness

We can receive
The passion and guidance
To pray and minister
By word and deed
All week

For so much secular
Can chip away, steer,
Veer away

And we get caught
In pathless brambles
Of tangled sorrows

Abba, please teach us
Lord, please tell us
In church and on paper

For whom and how to pray
What our missions, ministries
Outside the stained windows
Of inspired liturgy

Walkway on Sunday

A fellowship of
Oak trees around our church
Sway in empathy

Biblical

Like Ezekiel's Vision – Ezekiel 1:16-21

A clock around many clocks a-rolling
Way above rooms, houses, streets and towns
A fleeting vision, hinting all is not bound
By calendar days or thoughts turning round

Greater the movement of history's ages
And greater still the eons on God's wristwatch
His plans grander than those we can hatch
So glibly, as if readying the moon to catch

Passover – Exodus: 11, 12; John 14:6

The Hebrew letter *chet* (ch)
Pictures a door
The little *yod* (i, y)
Is like a flame

Both letters together
Telegraph life (*chai*)

That was the notice
To the angel of death

That reasoning belief
In the God of life

Tell despair and heavy cares
To pass over

Messiah in the Bible

The woman cried for her daughter
The man begged for his son
Christ, the Lord of all
Healed them, every one

The people yearned for learning
The disciples worried about food
Christ, the Provider of all
Gave nourishment and good news

The blind man asked to see
The deaf person prayed to hear
The one once possessed by demons
Was freed from chains of fear

What other Messiah do we want?
Why throw bitter stones at His door?
When the Healer, Redeemer returns
Let's welcome Him as Lord and Savior

Keep Calm – Numbers 20:18

Just speak to it, Moses
Don't hit that rock
It has feelings, perceptions too

Let's all just
Depend on God
Not on our paradigm box
Not on our deadlining clocks
Not our training

And restrain
Angry impatience

Let Me Tell You – Luke 1

I have been told
By eyewitnesses
What happened,
Dear Theophilus

So let me relate
What came to pass
Starting from the days
Of Zacharias

The miracle that happened,
The announcement there
Made to Mary, the obedient
Innocent surrogate mother

For the Son of God
Jesus the Christ
Born to save us from ourselves
And offer eternal life

Rejoice, Theophilus
Give thanks to the Lord
Await further instructions
Keep reading, living His word

Luminosity

The lovely
Mysterious
Luminosity
Of the gospels

The good news
Of God Who descended
Into our few dimensions
Then rose as our
Redeemer

The biblical story
Haunts me
Comforts me

Into belief
Grateful worship
Of God

Lord of all,
The Truth,
The Way
And the Light

Needed for a ministering
Earthly time
And a joyous, heavenly
Eternal life

Mandated Gift

Sabbath, that wonderful
Torah-mandated gift
Of a work/rest program
Was so wisely, considerately
Established for us

To anticipate and enjoy
A holy, healing
Weekly celebration
No matter what

Good News

Good news for the heart
God has risen
With the sun on His wings

Good news for the soul
His love revives, heals
And makes us whole

Good news for those who intercede
Every prayer place can become a cathedral
With a land to heaven line

Good news for the spirit
Deep calls unto deep, yearnings are heard
And God does respond as you open

The windows of your hopes
To His answering word

Psalm 23 – The Lord is Our Shepherd

Thy rod and Thy staff
If placed at right angles
Somewhat in the shape of a cross

They comfort us, lead us
Set us free from despair
To walk in Thy paths
And do the right thing

Psalm 23 – Elaborated

The Lord is my Shepherd
    My teacher, Leader, Healer, Counselor, King

I shall not want
    Nor despair for
    Time, rest, fellowship or leadership

He makes me to lie down in green pastures
    Full of lovely flowers
    Even on this post-Edenic earth

He leads me besides still waters
    That he has separated like the Sabbath
    And His calm reigns all week

He restores my soul
    He cleanses my feet from the dust of the journey
    He strengthens my heart and renews my mind

He guides me in the path of righteousness
    With the amazing grace of His forgiveness,
    He orients my footsteps

For His name's sake
    With the mentorship of Christ,
    In the joy of His Holy Spirit
    For His honor, whose name is One

Even when I walk through the valley of the shadow of death
  Dug with the world's tears, chiseled with willful pollution
  Containing dinosaur bones of past mistakes that still trip us

I shall fear no evil
  Thou givest me courage and hope
  Thou defendest my soul

For Thou art with me
  Thou walkest many extra miles to reassure me
  Thou hast borne all sufferings to accompany me

Thy rod and Thy staff, they comfort me
  Thy chastisement and Thy hand restrain, retrain me
  Thy economy of circumstances
  Lead me back to Thee

Thou preparest a table before me
  Shulchan Aruch. Why Thou art so merciful, I can't understand
  Thy bounteous feast accords what I need and more

In the presence of my enemies
  Who have mostly become neighbors, friends, co-workers
  With more understanding, commonalities between us

Thou annointest my head with oil
 Washing away bitterness with Thy Holy Spirit
 Consecrating me for Thy service

My cup overflows
 My emotions segue into gratefulness
 Words cannot express my thankfulness

Surely goodness and mercy
 Thy love, comfort and truth
 Thy ingrained word

Will follow me
 Build the road for me
 Map the next steps with wisdom
 Remember the previous journeys

All the days of my life
 In my borrowed time
 Here on the third planet from the sun

And I will dwell
 And I will sing of Thy goodness with all instruments
 And I will praise Thee to the highest of my ability

In the house of the Lord
 In His many-roomed mansion
 Built with the cornerstone of salvation

For the length of days
 Ten thousand times ten thousand years
 And all the moments of forever

Sufficient – 2 Corinthians 12:9

– My grace is all you need
Think of My many unmerited gifts to you
– But, Lord, what about cruelties tragic
Suffering, sickness, death and terrible deeds

My love can and will shine through
Together with your faith and service
We can build bridges from fallen strongholds
To My land of peace, goodness and truth

Historical Priorities

Pharisees:

Answering a question with another question
Commenting on the commentaries
Discussing miniscule points of righteousness
And how our lives can God's holy name bless

Sadducees:

At this critical time we must criticize
It's better to be politic and wise
Towards the powers that be, so that we can
Help our traditions and hierarchies stand

Zealots:

No other way to gain our freedom
Than to be armed and ready to fight
How else can we survive present and future tests
To overcome our status of the helplessly oppressed

Jesus:

You're all sincere in your way
Yet witnessing wrongly if you stray
From the guidance of God above
With His forgiving, overarching love

If It Were

If the bible were written utterly by people
With their inclinations, needs and demands
Wouldn't biblical leaders more perfectly stand
And not all fall due to some carnality?

Wouldn't Moses have been shown to be
Not impatiently angry but wisely serene?
Would David's history be marred with sensual faults?
Would Solomon be reported as sacrificing to cults?

Would Peter so often have missed Jesus' call?
Would Paul have mourned
I want to do well, yet I fall?
Would John the beloved have fled for his life?
Would there have been so much interdisciple strife?

Recognizing our faults in theirs
We can see that God still cares
And how much He wants to redeem mankind
To write the bible with His hands intertwined

Tears in the Heart – Matthew 26:6-14

Jesus was always aware and truly cares
What we are thinking, saying, doing

They thought the alabaster jar had Pandora's name
Jesus saw faith in the woman's tearful heart

May all our judgements, expectations likewise be kind
Believing Thou canst every lost soul find

Truth and Grace Were Here – John 1:1-25

His shoelaces
We were no worthy to untie

He was the searching light
When we were lost in dark caves

He was truth and grace
And we actually saw His face

But neither being
Elijah nor a warrior Messiah

We did not understand
His sacrifice of love

O when will we ever see Him again
And wash with our tears His nail-scarred feet
And dry with our hair His outstretched hand

John 1:1, Martin Buber – *I and Thou*

In the beginning was the Word
In the beginning was the connection
Between the Creator and all created

So the Word is the connection
Witnessing an I-Thou relationship
Since sounds and words and language
Bring communication

And He
Who was nailed
To the cross of the world
Gave us the word
Of love

Matthew 21:14-16 – All Praise and Worship

The children shouted in the temple
Hosanna! Save us as we grow
Into the missions Thou hast for us
Help us serve only Thee in good trust

The impatient stones started to sing
Welcome to the Lord, Creator and King
We have been waiting for hardened hearts
To realize and declare how great Thou art

The mountains and hills began to dance
Do we recognize what creation is saying?
Lord, let us also give Thee glad praise
Praying for Thy glory, loving Thee always

Listen to the Rest of the Story

The burning bush was not consumed
The persecuted people were not destroyed
Souls were made to live forever
The tortured Christ was not killed

Look Around

Connections

Glass is sand
Molecules scurrying

Minutes are lives
Hours hurrying

Moods sometimes,
Form decisions
Roads choosing

Seasons are presents
Conversations starting

Families are countries
With diplomacies loving

Graces are marvels
Of God's mercies surprizing

Every atom sings
God's miracles witnessing

What's the Matter?

Matter is slow energy
Objects are just waiting
To form protective fortresses
Around thoughts and memories
In danger of escaping

Cenizo's Witness

Bursts of purple color
In my face
As I water
The yellowed lawn

The flowering *cenizo* beams
Look! How beautiful God made me
When I'm all dressed up

Sunset Too Ephemeral

Now how
Can I
Close the blinds
And walk away rudely

When the sunset
Is waving
A purple, gold, coral
Quick goodbye

Through grey feathery
Evening trees

A Hundred Hands

A hundred hands
Of soft green weeds
With tiny yellow flowers

Form a holding basket
Waiting to hand over
The morning newspaper

In formal, caring style

The Curtain Opens

A creaking metal horizontal curtain
Of a garage door
Opens

To an airy street vista
Sunbeams talking to trees and houses

All ready to start
The play of a day

Let's applaud
The Author – God

Shades

Look at the shading on the closet's door
Gradually darkening into the unlit room

You can close the door, to stop the shadow
Or turn the light on
Your perceptions and memories

Not forgetting to thank
The electricity / sun Maker

From a Hospital Window

The twinkling seas of city lights
The solemn processional waves of cars
The mauve waters of evening settling in
Lord, Thou art the Creator above all

The oceans of hills ringing the horizon
The sun writing his last colorful farewells
For this panorama, and many granted pleas
Lord, we thank Thee, Keeper of all

Behold

Shimmering rivers
Bees of gold
What beautiful riches
Our Father unfolds

Trees of silver
Skies deeper than blue
We could have many Edens
On an earth renewed

Amber sunsets
Life-painted art
Masterpieces
After God's own heart

Neighboring Rooftops

Let's celebrate, appreciate
The music, the talk, the silence
The sunshine and rain

Across red, tan, brown, gray
Neighboring rooftops beyond
Our pale and dark green hedges

And when we worry through
The hours, let not, must not
Insomniac depressions,
Impressions, illness, adversities
Even tragedies
Keep us away from, persuade us

Against Thy returning
Glorious blue skies

Not So Wild

Wildflowers
Like mauve *origami* papers
Fluttering

Wildflowers
Like yellow-pompomed cheerleaders
Joyously dancing

Wildflowers
Prim in their Easter bluebonnets
Congregating

Wildflowers
Painting the town red
Artfully

Wildflowers
In delicate bridal white
Musing

Wildflowers …
Laughing, dancing, musing
Painting, fluttering, congregating

Maybe those wildflowers
Aren't so wild
After all

Psalm 23 – To Contemplate the Lovely

The awe factor latent
In the DNA of our souls

Is often activated while
Looking outside
At His green pastures

As God leads us
Besides still waters

To contemplate the lovely
To participate in the beautiful

And fall asleep
In the cradle
Of wonder

One Corner

Flashlight
On a counter
In the night

A triangle of light
For dust particles
To sparkle and dance
Quietly

A particular beauty
That a painter
Could perceive
Frame and spotlight
For all of us
To admire

Some angles and colors
Textures and composition
In one corner
Of our world

Languages to Translate, Thoughts to Donate

The singing trees, the dancing sands
The swinging stars, the murmuring strands
The painted clouds, the witnessing birds
Are all languages that translate God's word

The sun by day and the moon by night
The diamonds of time shining bright
The constant kaleidoscope of impressions
God sent to appreciate His gifts of creations

Fabled memories, tabled sorrows
Portraited yesterdays, faith's tomorrows
Loads we can't carry, thoughts we can't understand
All can be given into God's wise hands

Two Painting Prompts

Greyish the drapes framing both paintings

Who are these ladies?
Each at their open windows

One looking outside to the beckoning horizon,
Blue wavelets, sailboat –
Refreshed, though maybe lonely

One with eyes closed against the heat, meditating
With a carelessly held rainbow ice-cream bar –
For an opportunistic puppy

Both ladies waiting
As we do in the forever still morning
For poems on angel wings

Gone Fishing

Fishing for right words
In waves of moving moments
That halt when they're found

Can Objects Witness Also?

Examining the archeology
Of silent objects you left behind

What pressures and stresses beset you,
O ancient predecessors?
What missives in the signs?

Did you leave suddenly, regretting
Work undone, lessons not learned?
Should we construct scenarios
Or leave those sparse clues unturned?

Let us pray for you, our sharing ancestors
That one day we'll joyfully meet
And sing together in the heavenlies
Holding hands with our mutual Father

What Do You See?

Windows
What do you see?

Cloud sailing over a chimney
What sweet breeze pushes thee?

Trees growing greenly, stalwartly
What talented hand formed thee?

Planet trying to survive patiently
May God's good will save thee
Divinely, miraculously

Prayers and Thanks

Let There Be

For mistakes, sadnesses
Let there be
Do-overs, redemptions

For good choices
Let there be
Blessings and thankfulness

For all
Let there be
Salvation and grace

O Lord, dear Lord

When Roads Seem to Stop

If computers are advanced typewriters
And our minds are glorified computers
Then, Lord, let our thoughts review
With tech old and new
Thy amazing graces and give Thee glory

If our dreams wake us up with songs
While their images
Still scurry in our memories
Please God, let us understand their signs
And how they solve some of our puzzling stories

If our occupations, missions and ministries
Are avenues of creative kindnesses
And they suddenly seem to stop

Then, Lord, help us over
The walls and speed bumps
To find new roads
With Thy constant mercies

Newcomer's Prayer

May this
City of hopes
Be inspirational for all
Where we riverwalk
Together
With the Creator

May
The golden dawns, angel clouds
Jewelled evenings, sparkling
Webbed wire networks carry
God's good words

May
The bluebonnetted hills
Lost maples, live oaks
And cedar trees
Connecting earth and sky
Help our wondering hows and whys
Reach for His hand, pray

God bless this place
And all people, lands
With His grace

Later Grace

The granted answers
To our much-raced-towards prayers
That we focused on so avidly

Sometimes come later
When we're on
Totally different tracks
Pursuing newer goals

That segue
Into farther rainbows

That keep receding
Before our wishing eyes

But that's to be acknowledged
Gratefully also

Your Lives Matter Infinitely

Afflicted, victimized ones
Imprisoned, choked, enslaved
Shot, terrorized, robbed, killed
Tear-gassed, tasered
Persecuted

Your lives matter infinitely
Everyone has been diminished,
We are sickened with your suffering
Your shocks, pains, losses
Are also our tragedies

Let's pray together
That God helps us all
Protecting, leading us
To become truly caring
Supportive neighbors

And please send us
Wise, humble and kind leaders
We can trust

Losses

Such dear, sweet souls
Gone through the door
Of our world
Lord, please
Welcome them
Into heaven

Thou knowest our hearts' prayers
Let their spirits walk joyously with Thee
And be forever nurtured and blessed
And friended graciously

Thanks for Our Poetry Sessions

Noting
An unusual absence or tardiness
We were waiting, reserving
Our friend's usual seat

When
We should have been praying
Commemorating

For
We were actually
Keeping the space
For a ghost

Since
He had died
A ways back

Taking with him
His congenial talk,
Referenced readings,

Flute, cane
And pencilled poems

May his soul
Joyously talk
With his ancestors

And participate
In awesome poetry sessions
In heaven with many
And with Thee

Whom Do We Thank?

What strange constructs
Deemed marvelously benevolent
Are sought, praised
And thanked

Serendipity, synchronicity,
Good fortune, providence,
Wonderful luck
Or rewardable merit

While really Thou, Abba
Art the One Who
Shepherds us on good paths

How lovely are Thy pastures
The sparkling, marvelous rivers
That quench our thirst
Soothe our souls
With true nourishment

Give us the graces, Lord
To recognize Thy miracles
And be grateful
To Thee

Word File

Still in computer
Despite my user error
Thanks, God, so tech-wise

Circle of Love

Family,
Circle of love
Brave survivors
Safe lives fostering
Adjusting, learning

Family,
Circle of love
Wonderful
Husband, son, daughter,
Flourishing, learning
In the Rio Grande Valley
Finding Thee, Lord God, there
And above

Family
Circle of love
Here in the Texas Hill Country
Now with amiable
In-laws friended
Grandkids amazing
Growing, learning

Such blessings
Such gifts of grace
Such miracles

More than
Mere happenstance
Greater than good fortune

From Thee, Lord God
Thine be
Thanks, honor and glory

Bouquet

Every flower is a universe
Of colorful, inimitable patterns
Each leaf has its highways of veins
Busily transporting nourishment

Each room is a world
Of rhythm and style, comfort and decorations
Each house has its message
Commenting corners, architectural meditations

Every person can be a rainbow
Of good goals and quests, true views and prayers
May everyone receive a bouquet
Of flowers, blessings and healing care

If / Then

If
Even the weary, sick and downtrodden
Could think of others and pray

If
Some would
Walk among enemies
Speak in their language
Address their cares

If
Jesus could redeem
The cross of
Fallen human nature

Then we can
Carry our burdens
Plead for others' salvation
And thank Him for His good grace

To Share, To Remember

Share
The wafers and juice
The bread and cider
The corn and wine

May the sacraments
Remind you
Of His loving
Gifts of grace

Let the Lord walk with you
Speaking words of comfort and life
Joyous, everlasting and true

www.ingramcontent.com/pod-product-compliance
Lightning Source LLC
Chambersburg PA
CBHW051824040426

42447CB00006B/364

* 9 7 8 1 6 3 0 6 5 1 3 3 6 *